"Thy Mind Never Sleeps, Thoughts of the Deep

Crystal Stevenson

Presentation by *BookLeaf Publishing*

Web: www.bookleafpub.com

E-mail: info@bookleafpub.com

ISBN: 9789360946555

First edition 2024

ACKNOWLEDGEMENT

Thanks to Book Leaf Publishing for the opportunity to participate in "The Write Angle " writing challenge". I appreciate the encouragement to keep writing and creating. I'm thankful for all the poets and writers that paved a way for myself and others with the gift to create masterpieces that will last a lifetime. Thanks to my mentors for believing in my ability to create compelling art through writing. Much thanks and gratitude to my support team, my lovely family for always being there cheering me on.

PREFACE

When there is silence,
Thy mind begins to speak and wonder,
There you will take a journey,
Into the underlying definition of the phases of Life,
Different stages of the memories as they come back synchronizing,
Like a whirlwind when you are deep in thoughts,
These are the constant translating voices that lies near,
With the power to stay trapped,
Trapped inside the experience of a moment within a day,
Anticipating the inclined perception be profound and intriguing,
Perplexed reflexes transparent universal waves without confinement

Thinkin of U

Thinkin of U early in the mornings,
 In the afternoon, in the evening,
  And deep in the night
      Thinkin of U

Thinkin of U when I smell the fresh air,
Watching the clouds form, in the sky,
While the birds fly high,
      Thinkin of U

Thinkin of U when the room gets quiet,
And sounds of your voice speaks in my mind,
So loudly talking to me,
Making it not so silent in this room,

Thinkin of U

Love For You

I love more than words can say,

I don't know why, you push me away,

Your flaws and all I want to stay,

Be who you are with me,

Never be afraid never shy away,

The love I have for you is more than the eyes can see,

Deeper than the sea and the ocean,

Nothing can change the love I have for you

Life Lost by Heartbreak

See how you moved,
Wished you wouldn't have played me tho,
You brought the soft spot out of me,
      Damn, why you fooled me,
Like we were a true fairytale, like in the movies,
      Put me on mute and laugh at me,
Say I'm stupid, give me the silent treatment,
 Cut me off my heart stopped beating,
      Now I'm lookin in this mirror like a fool,
Stabbed in the heart got me bleeding out,
 left for dead,

Blood all over the floor,
Pulse slowly fading as the clock ticks,
Body turning pale and purple, coldness sets in,
Another life lost to the puncture wound
inside the heart,
Life lost by Heartbreak

Loneliness

Raindrops pourin on the rooftop
water seepin thru the cracks in the ceiling

Drip Drip Drip Drip Drip, water drippin none
stop
constantly, the sound echoing thru the
house

No laughs, no voices
Only raindrop noises

No television playin
Only inner thoughts weighin

No lights on shinin
Only darkness behind these walls

No footsteps down the hall
Only quietness revolves

No faces to see
Only loneliness settin in me
Only loneliness waitin for me
Only loneliness comin to me
Only loneliness in my reach

Don't

Don't run from your fears, when they catch up
with you,
  you will be too tired to fight,

 Don't run from your nightmares,
they will always haunt you in the night air,

Don't run from your pain,
 face it to heal so your soul can be still,

Don't run from your worries,

they will always appear when it quiet and
boring,

Don't run from your dreams,
they are not far as it seems,

Don't run from your light,
you must shine bright,
when there's no light in sight,

Don't run from your Destiny,
everyday is a test to teach a lesson,
to look deep and find your reflection

Can't Let Go

This unreal I just can't, I just can't let go, what
happened to our love that was suppose to grow.
 You be on bullshit, you got us on standby.
Now you acting like you don't know what the
problem is, not blaming you or nobody for
nothing, your actions say another story.
 Contemplating, to say Fuck It All, why did I let
my feelings get involved?
 People show you where their heart and loyalty
belongs.

Tired of being overlooked or dropped in an
instant, sick of this treatment.
 My heart with you I never overlooked you.
Refuse to ignore you or runaway from you.
Profoundly, you the closet to heaven I ever been,
with you we can live in this life of sin.
 Killing me slowly deep within,

 I just can't let go you buried within

Life's Truth

Never meant to hurt no one, do what I can to make it better,
 just seems like I make it worse,
Grateful to help allot of people, at least I done some right in this lifetime,
 Wished to finish remarkable things that was started,
 instead of impulsively thinking I was incapable or not good enough,
 steady losing focus forgetting my wants and needs,
 just have hope with faith knowing it will be a greater way,

pay attention to my mission, change myself, be
attentive,
 to my actions and what's put in the universe,
been too negative many days, trouble never far
away, life just been really hard to consume,
 some people have it harder, guess that just how
it is I assume,
life is just a vision ultimately dimmed with
gloom....

Lessons

So exhausted rolling on the edge,
 stressing over situations out of my control,
Deep depression explode in my brain, hurt in my
soul, got me out of range,
 all the wild thoughts, got me feeling kinda
strange,
how to tame the evil, I'm so ashamed,
of the evil I desire to restrain, sit back an smoke
on pain reliever,
 life trying to kill me, grim reaper, maybe the
sun shine after the rain,

lookin in da mirror at the pain in my eyes, the
lessons was only gain in disguise, nothing will
never be the same, possibly I'm the one to
blame, never saw life as a game, just keep it real
an strongly maintain,
 from situations that make you go insane , like a
bullet lodged inside your brain

Dear Momma

I always love you, I miss your hugs how they be
so tight,
 like you didn't want to let go, cause you knew
you had to let go,
 the way you laughed and made jokes , how as a
little girl walking to stores you'll tell me to keep
you while holding my hand, I miss how you
warm my feet, when I was cold, how you took
care of me when I was young and old, how you
would always make homemade medicine tonic,

when I had a cold and sick, I miss on the
weekends as child we ride in the country and to
our favorite spots, we always loved going to the
park , you buy me coloring books and kick ball
with food packed with good treats, you shared
with everyone one at the park we meet, your
smile and kind personality always warmed
everyone heart, Single mother raising a son and
daughter, many days you did all you could even
though we struggled, You made the best meals
everything was made from scratch, always had
a delicious dessert to match, Everyday, you
made sure we had a hot plate, I miss the smell of
you cooking all of that, I know life wasn't
always kind to you so many missions you had to
go through, crying to yourself fighting without
no help, I would make you cards with poems
just to show you I care, even when you took
your last breath, I will always and forever be
there. I miss you but I knew you couldn't stay,
everyday a tear drop slowly from my face. Dear
Momma, I miss your warm embrace, I
understand you in a better place

Warrior

Awesome, Powerful, Captivating,
    he knew what he had to do to survive in
this world,
    a league of his own, protective ,
guarded, expressive, uncanny,
    extreme individual, he understands his
true desires,
    he walked with grace , integrity,
dignity, posed with much knowledge,
    he is incredibly wise and précised,
taking his own advice,
    overcoming all the situations that
attempt to stop him,
    he could never be held down nor
stopped,

for he is courageous in every battle he
fought,
holding everything in that he was
taught,
never surrender or retreat,
he understood the fortune of defeat,

Conversation between Mind and Body

Sitting here thinking mind talking to body,
Body, why haven't you moved,
Body, what are you waiting on,
Can you see that everything is waiting for you,
Body, why are you stuck in a zone,
Get up and receive what's already there for you,
Body, I won't be with here with you too long,
Body, I have a purpose of my own,
Use me now cause someday we both will be
gone,

We both know days don't last that long,

Goddess

I am a Goddess not a one-night stand,
I am a Goddess not a call up,
I am a Goddess not a down bitch,
I am a Goddess not a gutter bitch,
I am a Goddess not a quick fix,
I am a Goddess not a cheap trick,
I am Greatness,
I am Intelligent,
I am full of wealth,
I am great in health,
I am a Goddess, call me nothing more or
nothing less,

Vision

Pain in my mind
Love in my heart

Dreams in my hands
My soul in a trans
Light in my eyes
Bright is my sight
I know what is wrong
I know what is right
The dreams always occur deep in the night

She

All she really ever needed was love, an all she got was pain,

Tears fall from her cheeks, as a sharp pain goes
thru her heart,
Mourning the past loses, thinking her life was
supposed to be different from what she is seeing
of her reflection,
She hides and keep it all with a smile, no one
really by her side to
understand the things she tried to hide,
She endures all the consequences for her actions
an others,
She feel, sees, and knows their pain, yet, no one
feel, hears, or even care about her pain,
Hurt turn into sadness, sadness turn into pain,
pain turns into anger,
Yet, She still remain

Meant to Be

We got a special connection,
nobody can change that
when he going thru rough times, he know I got
his back
People wonder how we stay so close
We just built like that we from a different breed
We just built like that we grew from different
seeds
We built like that we are the Ultimate Dream
We built like that we are meant to Be;

Pleasure

U had me sprung since the first day I met you,
we united, we was together in the past, beautiful
love that was one,
We found a way back to each other,
U know its great to be in your presence, I savor
every moment with you,
Something so precious an sweet, yet strong and
protective,
I can taste you on my lips,
Kissing your body, while you moan,

Pleasuring you turns me on,
Wet like a fountain my love rain down on you,
Pounding inside of me, screaming your name so
loudly,
We make each other explode,
we take each other to the unknown;

Nothing is Something

Nothing is something,
even the floors desire to be
mopped,

the grass desires to get mowed,
the trees desire to get groomed,
the clothes desire to get fold ,
Everything is something,
even the walls desire to be cleaned,
Everything is something,
there's no such thing as Nothing

My Hometown

It use to be silence,
Now all I see is violence,
You hate me I hate you,
We use to be from the same crew,
You paid dues,
I paid dues,
Take me back to the old skool,
With the pro tools,
No young fools,
You know who,
This is a place ,

where Dreams are sold,
Lies are told,
The truth is about to unfold,
 You keep putting your life on hold,
 For things you need to let go,
Steady losing control,
Yet you know,
Don't fear,
Yet you think its Crystal Clear,
 The end is near,
We are here
Now we all shedding tears in My Hometown

HURT

Where did we go wrong, what have we done to
each other, how did it come to this
It use to be so much love an life full of forever
bliss, you would hold me in yours an say it will
be
ok with your kiss
Now its silence and arguments no more love
kindled moments, where did we go wrong
The smiles we use to share an the closer we use
to be, we made light in the darkness
When night would fall we would sit beneath the
Stars an Moon hoping our love wouldn't end
too soon
Now lately we just sit in the room not many
hugs and playfulness, where did we go wrong
The love we had use to be so strong, now these
four walls be so lonely
Oh how I miss my best friend the smell of your
skin and how sweet you taste
The infection of your laughter with so much
affection, there's no way your vibe could be
resisted
Now you gone ran away from home
Never realized pain can last this long

Unknown

Notes to the unknown word that's unspoken
buried deep to the core inside sealed away
Visions that have been foreseen but yet forgotten
Thoughts that have hidden beneath the surface
Uncontrollable images emerge threw smoke and
mirrors
Blurry paths that lead to detours within
destruction
Steps taken walking in purpose unseen obstacles
triumph and defeat
Pressure from gravity pulling inward,
Seeking validation from streams of guilty
conscience
Pursuing the greatest mission without harmful
intentions
Ambitions relevant to the journey running
through the tunnels
Searching constantly blindly in the darkness
Pacing vigorously with unmatched strength
Not knowing the destination but only the
purpose of living

Love Making

Caressing my body ohh, it feels so right, the way
you hold me tight makes me shiver from your
touch

Soft is your lips , your hands strongly touching
my hips with your firm grip
The warmth of your body on mines got my soul
intertwined
The smell of your skin takes my breath away
I lick my tongue slowly all over your body

You taste so sweet, your sweat dripping on my
legs as you grind in my body
None stop pleasure as I roll on top of you , yes,
moan as I open all your senses

With passion even have the Gods listening
Taking you to realms of ultimate heights
Filling me with all your love juices
We hold each other playing love music
We fall asleep together wrapped up in the covers

www.ingramcontent.com/pod-product-compliance
Lightning Source LLC
LaVergne TN
LVHW010918200726